W9-BFM-453

Creative Paper Art

Techniques for Transforming the Surface

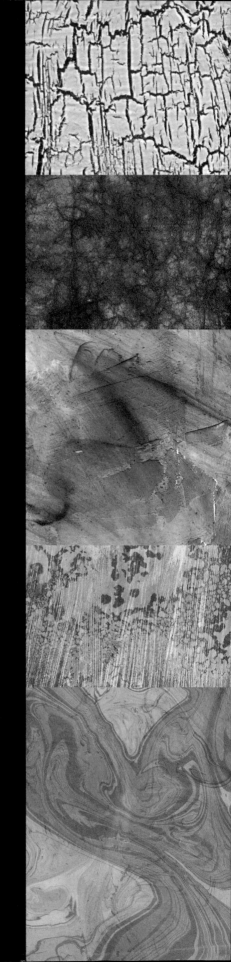

Creative Paper Art

Techniques for Transforming the Surface

by Nancy Welch

Sterling Publishing Co., Inc. New York
A Sterling/Chapelle Book

Chapelle Ltd.

Owner: Jo Packham

Editor: Linda Orton

Staff: Marie Barber, Ann Bear, Areta Bingham, Kass Burchett, Rebecca Christensen, Holly Fuller, Marilyn Goff, Shirley Heslop, Holly Hollingsworth, Sherry Hoppe, Shawn Hsu, Susan Jorgensen, Pauline Locke, Barbara Milburn, Karmen Quinney, Leslie Ridenour, Cindy Stoeckl

Photography: Kevin Dilley, photographer for Hazen Photography

Photo Stylist: Peggy Bowers

Acknowledgments: A huge bouquet of appreciation to friends who shared ideas and information — especially Barbara Hewitt, Linda Powers, Melissa Slattery, Mary Conners, Loretta Chance, and other artists whose work appears in this book. And Ned, dear, thanks for letting me have the new computer and for our more than forty years.

Library of Congress Cataloging-in-Publication Data

Welch, Nancy.
    Creative paper art : techniques for transforming the surface / Nancy Welch.
        p.   cm.
    Includes index.
    ISBN 0-8069-9457-6
    1. Paper work. 2. Decorative paper.   I. Title.
TT870.W437 1998   98-34946
745.54--dc21   CIP

10 9 8 7 6 5 4 3 2 1

A Sterling/Chapelle Book

Published by Sterling Publishing Company, Inc.
387 Park Avenue South, New York, NY 10016
© 1999 by Chapelle Ltd.
Distributed in Canada by Sterling Publishing
c/o Canadian Manda Group, One Atlantic Avenue, Suite 105
Toronto, Ontario, Canada M6K 3E7
Distributed in Great Britain and Europe by Cassell PLC
Wellington House, 125 Strand, London WC2R 0BB, England
Distributed in Australia by Capricorn Link (Australia) Pty Ltd.
P.O. Box 6651, Baulkham Hills, Business Centre, NSW 2153, Australia
Printed in China
All Rights Reserved

Sterling ISBN 0-8069-9457-6

The written instructions, photographs, designs, patterns, and projects in this volume are intended for the personal use of the reader and may be reproduced for that purpose only. Any other use, especially commercial use, is forbidden under law without the written permission of the copyright holder.

Every effort has been made to ensure that all of the information in this book is accurate. However, due to differing conditions, tools, and individual skills, the publisher cannot be responsible for any injuries, losses, and/or other damages which may result from the use of the information in this book.

If you have any questions or comments or would like information about any specialty products featured in this book, please contact:

Chapelle Ltd., Inc.
PO Box 9252
Ogden, UT 84409

Phone: (801) 621-2777
FAX: (801) 621-2788
e-mail: Chapelle@aol.com

Nancy Welch, author of several craft books believes that,

Even those of us that would rather make art than jams and jellies must maintain a semblance of household propriety. That is to say we can't completely stuff the kitchen cupboards with art supplies, there has to be things like flour, sugar, a little food coloring, and of course, brown paper bags, so the neighbors think you actually go to the grocery store. A bottle of bleach is also a good sign that you really care about keeping "the house clean." Nancy has a Masters Degree in Art which prompts her husband of 45 years to always ask before tasting anything. If you visit her you will find all these products neatly in their place, but if you visit when her four grandchildren are around, or you read this book, you will find out what these products are <u>really</u> for.

This book is dedicated to all those who would rather play than cook and clean.

Noni, Callie, Tanner, Sam, and Mac, never stop making art.

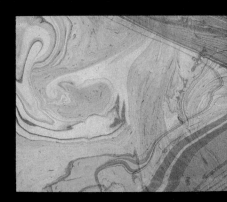

Paper is one of the least expensive craft materials and, in many cases it is free. What is more, it is easy to transform, using simple tools and techniques — even for those of us who feel limited by time, space, or talent. Whether you are looking for a way to amuse children or to enhance a serious art project, the ideas in this book are for you. The techniques, which require little equipment or supplies, are designed to inspire your creativity. You may wish to have more advanced instructions on a particular technique later on, but for now, dig in and have fun.

Craft techniques generally start with a long list of supplies. However, right this minute — stashed away in a drawer somewhere — you probably have everything you need to decorate paper. As you read through this book, you will find materials you may want to buy; but you can get started now by gathering up what is already on hand. Food coloring, ink, ink pads, and marking pens are all sources for color. Diluted household bleach brushed on some types of colored paper causes amazing results. Canning salt or rubbing alcohol sprinkled on wet water –based color adds pattern and texture. Paper soaked in tea or coffee instantly becomes "antique."

The type of paper used will obviously affect your results. Art supply stores, college bookstores, and commercial paper stores offer a variety of

Faux mud–cloth, using bleach (above). Stamped with bleach (middle). Photo soaked in tea (bottom right) by Alison Betts. Canning salt and alcohol sprinkled on wet watercolored paper (bottom left).

*I*ntroduction

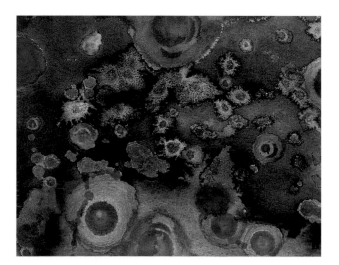

papers. Begin, however, by using whatever papers you have around the house. Be clever in your thinking. Look creatively, paper is everywhere. Do not overlook brown paper bags, paper towels, or newspapers. Newspaper want ads or foreign language newspapers can add interest. Recycle what you can — a clear, peel–off plastic cover from a new coffee maker produces the most wonder-ful "fog" over another paper. Scraps from the paper cutter are handy, too, for blocking and blotting paint. If a heavy–weight paper is need-ed, laminate five to six sheets together and you will have a piece of matt-board. View every piece of paper in a new, imaginative way.

Salt on watercolored paper; crackled metallic paint; marker over newsprint; and masking tape rubbed with shoe polish (top to bottom).

The color, texture, and absorbency of papers will determine which techniques work and which do not. Marker ink is crisper on glossy stock, but the ink used in Suminagashi works best on soft, absorbent paper. The ideas in this book look entirely different when used on colored paper. Keep all your decorative papers. Use those you do not like as a background for another technique, or cut them up for gift cards. Layer colors and tech-niques for a more interesting result.

Covering your finished papers with wax or specialty finishes, such as a crackle finish, com-pletely changes the appearance of the paper. Do not discount shoe pol-ish. It comes in a variety of colors, including gold, and looks just as great on paper as on your footwear. Create a faux leather finish by applying cut or torn strips of masking tape to a piece of heavy paper and rubbing with shoe polish.

Experiment and explore. This is when the fun begins, and this is how you make each piece unlike anyone else's, which is the way it should be when creating art. Perhaps the greatest reward about trans-forming paper surfaces is that you create the rules. Write a note on your first piece of decorated paper that says, "I am an artist. I make the rules!"

"Red Kimono" paper tube

For a bride, we are apt to think "something old, something new, . . ." For color, think something light, something bright, something neutral, and something dark. Color can set the mood from bright and happy to somber or sophisticated. Color conveys just about any effect you want to create. Numerous books have been written about the psychology of color and how to use it. Here are a few elementary strategies:

✦ All colors can be described by defining hue or color name, value or lightness and darkness, and intensity or the strength of a color. Create variety within an overall color scheme by choosing hue, value, or intensity to provide a dominant area of accent or contrast. The proportion will affect the overall effect. Generally, different hues of the same value blend together more easily than do sharply contrasting values.

✦ To jazz up a color scheme, include a tiny bit of the complementary color, such as red to green or orange to blue, with your dominant color.

✦ To make a light color appear brighter, place it against a dark background of the complementary color — yellow will appear brighter next to purple than if placed next to orange.

✦ Use intermediate hues to connect widely contrasting ones. Tie dull red and bright yellow together by using a midvalue orange.

✦ There is no right or wrong on how you use color. Color use is a product of both fashion and tradition; heredity and environment.

✦ Cultural groups use color very differently. Carefully observe Persian carpets, Tibetan rugs, Japanese woodblock prints, Indian textiles, Scottish tartans, Mexican folk art, African masks, and Chinese porcelains. Investigate colors from different art periods, such as the American Art Deco colors from the 1920's. Where you live affects the colors you select. American Southwest artists choose a different color palette than their counterparts in the Pacific Northwest.

✦ Train yourself to see color by really looking. Inspect leaves and flowers, notice how many colors are actually present. Is the sky just one shade of blue or the earth just one shade of brown? Notice how the colors are distributed. A purple pansy may have tiny bits of green and yellow as complementary colors.

✦ Nature is a fine teacher, but so are art books, prints, and museums. Examine colors throughout history. Compare the Gobelin tapestries with Coptic textiles, Matisse with Renoir, Rubens with El Greco, or the colors of Napoleon's empire with the Victorian period.

Using Color

◆ Color is not seen in isolation, it is affected by the the others around it. Prove this by putting a gray–blue shape on other hues and notice how the apparent color of the shape changes. When gray is placed on other colors varying in value and intensity, it will change dramatically.

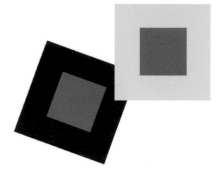

A young Korean college student, newly arrived in the United States, wrote this about color:

This afternoon I walked around campus to find my favorite color. Here, it is very easy to find the green. For me, I like blue better than green. While I was walking around here and there, I found a lot of blue things. Three of my classmates were in blue. I think people think the blue as the summer's color. Why they think the blue as the summer's color? Maybe it would be a personal question. I found the blue from somebody's car, my socks, and inside of the U.S. flag. Now, I would like to say my feelings about the blue. Someone say the water cannot have a specific color. Whenever I think of water, I think it can change its color and its own shape. It symbolizes flexibility. Once it is frozen, it can melt in the air. I want to change my fixed personality like the blue water does.

Plate, paper–découpaged underneath by Deborah Waimon.

chapter one

The following ideas, techniques, and materials can be used to create a variety of designs and backgrounds from book covers and endpapers, to setting off rubber stamping, calligraphy, or a letter to your mother.

Many of the materials and supplies used in this chapter are common household products that you may already have on hand.

Sponging

Sponging is a quick way to eliminate white backgrounds, fill in open areas, or blend colors. Varying type and texture of the sponge, altering dampness, and amount of paint used influences the final effect.

Cosmetic sponges, sponge brushes, and natural sponges are all perfect for this technique. Even a foam ball can be pressed into service, or use your fingers wrapped with foam packaging. The foam packaging can also be gathered at the edges and secured with a rubber band to form a paint dauber. Ink a rag and dab or roll it onto paper.

Use a water–based paint product, such as acrylic, watercolor, poster, or house paints. Color may also be applied to your sponge, using watercolor markers, ink, or ink pads. Protect your fingers by holding the sponge with a spring–loaded paper clip, an alligator clip, or suture clamps.

Basic sponging technique by Rhonda Rainey.

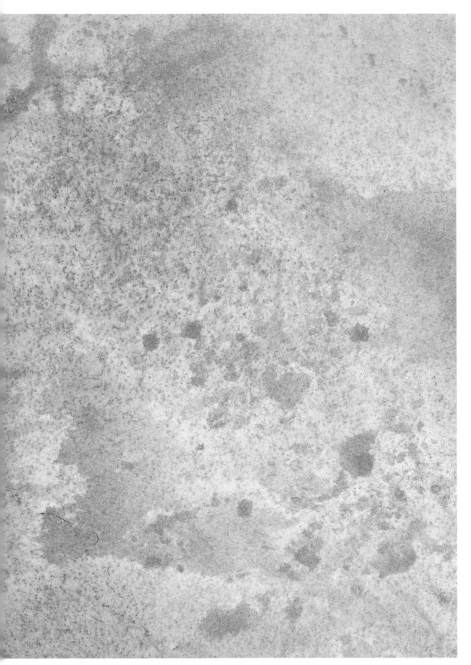
Basic sponging technique.

Basic technique

Dip a sponge into a small amount of paint and dab onto the paper. Add additional colors over the first color to give more depth. Blot the edges of stiff sponges on scratch paper before printing to diminish lines. *Note: Avoid edge lines by cutting off the sponge edges with pinking shears or by folding them under.* Fold the sponge edges under to form a ball, and use as a smooth paint dauber. Keep a spray bottle handy and lightly mist the sponge to create watercolor effects, or drag a dry sponge across the surface to reveal the paper underneath.

Tips/Hints:
✦ If you apply too much paint to your paper, sponge off the extra.

Exploring the technique

✦ Sponge through stencils, lace, loose–weave fabric, or thicker materials like berry baskets to add pattern.

✦ Use a sponge as a paintbrush by inking with a marker, dipping in paint, or pressing on an ink pad, then sliding the sponge across the paper surface.

Metallic paint sponged onto dark background.

✦ Apply several colors to your sponge, press on the paper, and twist your wrist to swirl a rainbow.

✦ Dab an inked, rough sponge onto the paper to create texture. For smooth–looking surfaces, glide a dense sponge across the paper to blend colors.

✦ To achieve an airbrush effect, apply color with a marker to center of sponge, avoiding the edges. Blot the sponge on scratch paper.

✦ Fold the sponge in your hand until smooth and round, then lightly dab over artwork. Build up areas of color by varying pressure.

✦ For a furry effect, use the middle of your sponge and apply more pressure.

✦ Dab metallic paint onto an open–celled sponge to add "stars" to dark paper.

Sponged paper torn and découpaged onto painted background overlaid with stenciled pattern by Rhonda Rainey.

✦ Create spirals by twisting an inked sponge on paper.

✦ For an "impressionist" effect, apply color to a rough, natural sponge and lightly dab onto the paper. Apply other colors and fill in around first application. *Note: Colors may bleed together if first color is still wet.*

✦ Create a cloudy sky by cutting a cloud shape from paper and sponging around the edges with gray paint. Vary the density to yield effects ranging from wispy to fluffy. Move the shape and fill in the sky with more clouds.

✦ Cut the sponge into any shape and use for printing.

✦ Sponge layers of ink onto the paper ending with the darkest color on top. Lightly mist the surface with window cleaner. Where the solution is applied, the upper color layer will disappear.

✦ Use ink pads for sponging. They come in small plastic containers with oval, square, and round sponge heads. Since they are already inked, dab them lightly.

✦ Deliberately apply a layer of paint and remove with a stiff–bristled brush, dry rag, or sponge.

Spattering

Spattering is effective in creating an all over pattern or in highlighting a specific area on your paper. The spattering technique is done by filling a stiff brush with paint and tapping the handle or scraping the bristles to spatter the paint. The size of the paint droplets will depend on the amount of paint on the brush, how hard you tap or scrape, and the distance between the brush and the surface. The design can be spattered before or after embellishments are added. You can be exuberant and fling the paint, or scrape softly for an elusive mist.

Basic spattering techniques.

Basic technique

Gather up a paintbrush (a toothbrush, or a nailbrush may be substituted) and a scraper tool, such as a small screen, cardboard, stick, or knife. Tools designed specifically for spattering, such as a speckling tool that resembles a mini bottlebrush with a handle that twists, can be purchased at the craft store. The ultimate spatterer is an airbrush, but getting involved with a compressor and airbrush equipment can be expensive.

Cover the work area with plenty of newspapers to catch any flying paint. Place your paper on top of the newspaper away from anything you do not want spattered, or in a cardboard box set on its side to keep the airborne particles from traveling. Dab the brush in a small amount of paint, shake off excess onto the newspaper. The thicker the paint, the more distinct the spatters will be. Spatter by loading the brush with paint, then tap the handle as you move the brush over the surface; using a scraper tool, pull the bristles of the brush toward you; or hold a screen parallel to the paper and drag the brush toward you across the screen. Experiment with the distance between the screen and the paper to distribute the spatters. *Note: Avoid overloading the brush before scraping so paint will not splatter in globs.*

Basic spattering technique.

Exploring the technique

✦ Spattering can be done over stencils or masked and blocked out areas.

✦ Mask off areas on the paper with scrap paper and spatter different colors onto each section. Allow the color to dry before spattering on your next color.

✦ Spatter all types of mediums, from household bleach to metallic paints, white gesso to clay mud.

✦ Be as wild as the medium will allow. Use many colors, or try subtle color–on–color, such as white spatters on white paper.

✦ A similar effect can also be achieved with a fine–mist spray bottle or atomizer filled with diluted ink or paint. Before spraying, tape the paper to a slanted board to prevent puddles. Spray lightly to avoid drips. This simulates airbrushing with much less cost but also much less control.

Brayer Inking

Unless you are a print–maker, you may not have a brayer stashed in a drawer. It looks and works like a miniature paint roller. Brayers are available in several sizes at art stores. A new, smooth, soft brayer works best, but worn brayers can produce some very interesting textures. Inexpensive sponge or foam rollers from paint stores are worth trying but give a lighter and softer finish.

Ink brayered over skeletonized layered leaves by Michiko Toyama.

Basic technique

Roll the brayer over a single-colored or a multicolored ink pad. When using a multicolored pad, always start the roller at the same spot to keep colors clean.

Roll the brayer over the ink pad until all surfaces of the roller are saturated with color. Roll the brayer over the paper several times until the surface is covered. Re-ink the brayer and continue to roll until the color is smooth and even.

Create an ink pad by folding a paper towel and placing it in a waterproof container, such as a styrofoam meat tray. Pour water-based ink or food coloring onto the paper towel.

Tips/Hints:
✦ A multicolored rainbow ink pad can be made by purchasing stamping inks in desired colors and a blank pad. Apply colors in parallel lines the length of pad.

✦ Clean your brayer by running the roller over a dampened rag, such as an old sock or an absorbent cloth, and rolling onto scratch paper until the ink is removed.

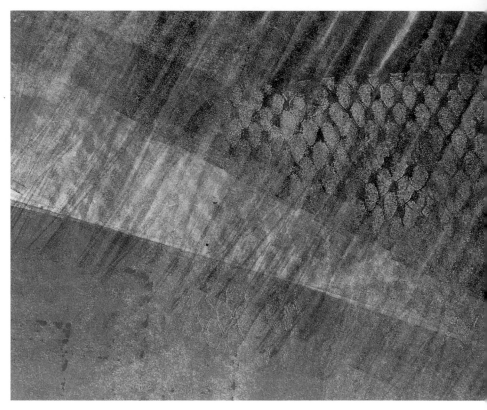

Brayered ink background with metallic paint brayered over fabric mesh.

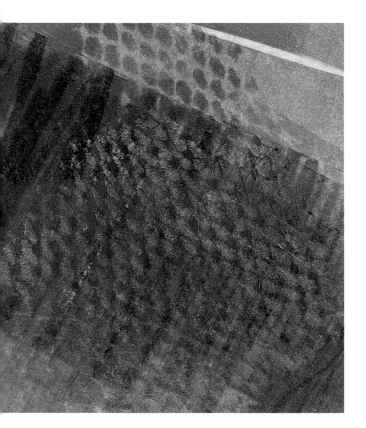

Exploring the technique

✦ For a watercolor effect, wet the brayer and roll it over the ink until the colors blend together, or roll clear water onto the paper first, then brayer on the color.

✦ Create plaids by rolling the brayer over part of the paper, leaving some surface areas white. Turn the paper ninety degrees and roll the brayer in the opposite direction. Plaids can also be created by blocking out areas on the paper with removable tape or strips of scrap paper. Roll on the first color, remove the tape, then roll on the second color.

✦ Draw designs on the brayer roller with watercolor markers and roll instant graffiti onto paper. Draw straight or curvy lines, dots, and dashes around the roller. Designs can be drawn on the roller, using a ruler or freehand.

Outline the pattern with a black pen to make your designs more distinctive.

✦ Some brayers have removable rollers that will allow cellophane, string, or rubber bands to be wrapped around the roller for printing textures and designs.

✦ Adhere shapes cut from felt, fun foam, or thin, unmounted rubber stamps onto the roller to make a rolling printer. Double-sided tape is a speedy way to attach shapes.

✦ Create interesting patterns and textures by rolling an inked brayer over a leaf, a stencil, a piece of raveled cheesecloth or nylon stockings, a net bag, a paper lace doily, shelf edging, or metallic paper leftover from making sequins. Roll the brayer over cut or torn shapes of newsprint, then remove paper shapes and allow the background to show through.

✦ Place a textured material under the paper, and roll the brayer over the surface to print the underlying texture.

Bubbling

Bubbling is a spontaneous and simple technique for creating a decorative paper surface. Bubbling is truly a kid–pleaser and safe even for toddlers.

Basic bubbling technique, using a round container and two colors.

Basic bubbling technique, using three colors by Tanner Welch, age 4.

Basic technique

Mix ½ cup of liquid detergent, bubble bath, or bubble–blowing solution with 1 cup of water in a container. The shape of your container will determine the shape of your bubble print. A round container will produce a round pattern and a square or rectangle pattern will be produced when using those container shapes. Mix a few drops of food coloring, water–based paint, or dye into your detergent solution. Place a straw in the mixture and blow until you have lots of color–laden bubbles. Make certain you have added enough color to saturate the water. Place the paper over the bubbles until it just touches the foam. The bubbles will burst and leave their colored imprint on the surface.

Exploring the technique

✦ Multiple colors can be applied to the surface by mixing a soap solution for each desired color. Try using blue food coloring to create a mottled sky and green to create a grassy field.

✦ Prepare a solution of metallic ink and detergent, then bubble it onto a dark paper surface.

Rubbing

Rubbing or frottage allows you to instantly reproduce any textured surface directly onto paper. Designs on everything from sewer covers to ancient carvings can be simply transferred by covering the relief surface with paper and rubbing gently with a soft-lead, colored, or wax-based pencil or crayon.

Soft pencils and graphite are excellent for rubbing, but they will smear unless protected by a clear fixative or a covering of clear contact paper. For a large project, use big child-sized crayons, crayon blocks, or a triangular block of wax used by shoe repairmen to buff out shoe scuffs. The great thing about frottage is there's no waiting — just rub a print and immediately rub another.

Rubbing with crayon over a New Guinea drum, then colorwashed.

Abbey rubbing with metallic crayon.

Basic technique

Place coins, doilies, or leaves under paper and rub with the long side of a crayon to pick up patterns. Use double–sided tape to secure the objects to the table if necessary. Or, take paper and crayons on your next walk around town and see what you can record by rubbing.

Tips/Hints:

✦ Paint a colorwash of watercolor, wood stain, or India ink over your completed wax rubbing. Wax can be ironed out, if desired.

✦ Make your own wax blocks by melting down old crayons in muffin tins.

✦ To keep the color in bounds, place a piece of cardboard against the edge of the design to catch errant strokes. To make a finished rubbing even neater; cut it out and mount it on separate paper.

Exploring the technique

✦ Take rubbings over folded, torn, or cut papers to create interesting designs.

✦ Take rubbings of rubber stamps.

✦ Take rubbings on black paper with metallic crayons.

✦ Buff finished rubbings with old nylon stockings to give a sheen.

✦ Be creative in the amount of pressure used. Add tonal qualities by rubbing harder in certain areas and lighter in others. The direction of the rubbing will influence the final print. Experiment, using pressure and direction to achieve the amount of dimension desired.

✦ Use an alternative rubbing technique by taping paper securely over a textured object, spraying lightly with water, and gently pressing the paper into the design with fingers. Let dry slightly. Tap the surface of the paper with an ink dauber or soft, ink-covered rag to highlight the design.

Rubbing with crayon over a New Guinea drum on handmade paper.

✦ Make permanent designs for rubbing by adhering cardboard shapes or other textures (rice, lentils, sandpaper, string) to a backing. Shapes can be overlapped to add dimension and interest. For example, add eyes, a nose, and whiskers to a cutout of a cat's head, or draw designs with thick craft glue on cardboard. When dry, place paper over the raised surface and rub to transfer the design.

✦ To include words, spell out a favorite sentiment, using rubber stamps. To repeat a saying, make a permanent block from pottery or polymer clay. Lightly press the letters into the clay, bake according to directions, and use the form to make a rubbing. The words will be recessed, but readable.

Tempera _Washout_

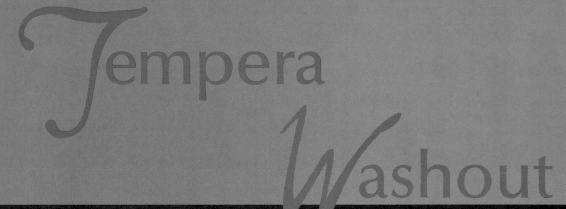

The paper produced using this technique is anything but a washout. Tempera or poster paint acts as a resist for waterproof ink. Permanent ink will not adhere to tempera paint. Black ink makes a nice contrast against bright paints.

Basic tempera washout technique by Robin Gandolfi.

Basic technique

Draw or print design with tempera paint onto heavy paper, cardstock, or cardboard. Lightweight paper cannot withstand the washing required to remove ink. After paint dries, brush painted surface with waterproof ink. When ink is dry, run water over paper to wash away ink. The areas where tempera paint was applied will appear.

Basic tempera washout technique by Gail Gandolfi.

Smoke Smudging

This is a great technique for creating a ghostly effect. But, beware, like a ghost, this surface design easily disappears with the slightest wear unless protected with a sealant.

Basic technique

Do this technique in the sink, or at the very least next to a bucket of water. Avoid coated paper because it may buckle or the smudging may wipe off; or lightweight paper because it will catch fire too easily. Light a candle and slowly move your paper back and forth or up and down over the candle flame. The paper has to be close to the flame to smudge, but not close enough to catch on fire. The design will appear on the underside next to the candle. Lifting the paper up and down over the flame creates a different pattern, and swirling the paper through the flame produces another effect. *Note: If your candle is smokeless or does not produce enough smoke, try using an old metal spoon or knife to cut through the flame to produce smoke.*

After smoke smudging, wait a few minutes for the smoke to set. The outer layer may still smear, so do not let it touch anything you do not want smudged. To preserve your pattern, lightly spray with hair spray, art fixative, or translucent spray sealant.

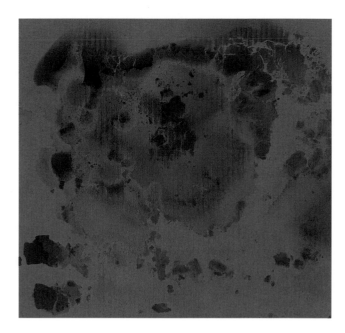

Smoke–smudged glue on paper (left page). Smoke–smudged wet paper (above).

Exploring the technique

✦ Run water over the surface after smudging to lighten the result.

✦ Smoke over or under pencil, crayon, water-color, or stamped designs.

✦ Smoke smudge on wet paper. When the smoke hits the water, it will fracture and make a speckled, marbled effect. Add watercolor or pearlescent acrylic paints to the water. Turn the wet paper over and swirl it through the flame. When nicely smoked but not dry, turn it right side up. Manipulate paper so the colored water runs and the smoked areas break up into interesting patterns.

✦ Create a glossy, almost metallic surface by coating a heavy piece of paper with a thick coat of craft glue. While the glue is still wet, smoke it in the flame. Allow glue to dry and buff off any soot. *Note: Craft glue can be thickened by temporarily placing in freezer.*

Smoke–smudged masks by Carol Stevens.

chapter two

Mildly Messy Techniques

The first part of chapter two uses many of the skills that you may have learned in kindergarten. Monoprints, and paste paper are grown-up names for fingerpainting. Remember when you smeared poster paint all over your desk, drew in it with your fingers, then put a piece of paper over it? The design transferred onto the paper and you took it home for mom to put on the refrigerator. You thought you were just having fun. No one told you that you had just made a monoprint. If there was starch mixed with the paint, you made

paste paper. It still feels just as good and is fun to do whether you are a child or an adult.

Other techniques include how to use faux finishes on paper surfaces, blueprinting, recycling paper bags, and dyeing.

Up to this point, most of the materials required for the different techniques can be found around the house. Some of the following procedures, especially those in the latter part of the chapter, may require a shopping trip.

Paste and marbling gift cards

Paste Paper

Paste–papers have been used for centuries as book end papers.

Some artists use rice or potato flour, some prefer wheat flour or cornstarch, while others mix different types of flour. Some artists like to cook flour and water, and others use paste paint without cooking.

Pigment may be added to the paste to color the design. Paste–paint recipes must be thick enough to manipulate and hold a design for paste paper. Metallic powder may be used alone in the paste or mixed into paste–paint to add radiance to the paper surface.

Paste paper pattern
#45 by Marie Kelzer.

Basic technique

Thick paint is necessary for paste paper. Mix water with acrylic, gouache, watercolor, or powdered tempera paint; then add liquid starch, wallpaper or library paste, white flour, or cornstarch to thicken. Blend until it is the consistency of a good mud–pie.

Try the four following **paste–paint recipes** and see which you prefer, or experiment to find your favorite recipe:

A. In sauce pan, mix 1 cup flour with 2 cups water to form paste. Add 2–3 cups water. Stir and cook until semitransparent. Add pigment of choice until desired color is achieved. Mix any combination of black, blue, red, yellow, or white pigments to obtain desired color. *Note: Colors will appear darker when wet.*

B. Place 3 cups of water in your blender, sprinkle 2 tablespoons of wallpaper paste (Methyl Cellulose) over water, and blend until smooth. Allow to stand for 30 minutes. Add 2 cups of water to blender mixture and whisk together until thoroughly mixed. Allow to sit eight hours, stirring occasionally. Add approximately 2 tablespoons of acrylic paint to 1 cup of paste. Add additional paint if necessary to achieve desired color.

C. Mix dry tempera paint with liquid starch.

D. Whip 1 cup of soap flakes, 1 cup of liquid starch, and 3 drops of desired food coloring to a creamy consistency.

Liquid detergent added to the paste makes it smoother, while glycerin keeps it from drying out too quickly. Start by mixing ½ teaspoon of detergent and ¼ teaspoon of glycerin into 1 cup of paste. Adjust the proportions as needed.

Choose strong paper that will withstand water and stress. Absorbent or handmade papers will not hold up. Experiment with colored papers. Small pieces of paper can be worked dry, but wetting paper with water first will keep the paste workable longer.

Use a sponge to dampen the paper or briefly submerge the paper in water; lift by diagonal corners, and let drain. If you are using large sheets of paper, roll them and briefly submerge them in a wallpaper pan of water. Lay the damp paper on a smooth, washable surface, such as plexiglass, glass, formica, or masonite. Sponge the damp paper until air bubbles are eliminated and it is affixed to the work surface. Remove excess moisture, using a sponge.

Paste paint on mylar.

Spread a layer of paste directly onto your paper with a wide, flat, foam or bristle paintbrush. Smooth and spread as evenly as possible. Several colors (that combine well together) can be applied next to each other. Make your design in the paste, using a sponge, comb, fork, pointed stick, dry paintbrush, square-notched adhesive spreader, fingers, or any other tool that occurs to you. Milk cartons, yogurt containers, old credit cards, or cardboard can be cut with pinking shears, decorative-edged scissors, or craft knife to make texturing tools. Faux-painting tools for furniture or rubber stamps add pattern, even a comb with missing teeth makes interesting lines. Draw straight or curved lines, intersect lines, or create grids for designs. Experiment and play in the paste. Designs are etched into the paste, revealing the color of the paper. Poke and play, being careful not to wear out your paper. If you do not like the design, simply smear on additional paste and begin again.

When your paste paper is finished, lift by the corners and place out of the way, or hang on a line until dry. Thicker paste will require a longer drying time. Dried artwork can be ironed on soft padding to set color and to smooth any wrinkles. If desired, rework with additional colors. Refrigerate leftover paste for up to one week.

Exploring the technique

✦ Remove paste paint to form a grid and make designs in each section.

✦ Try using light colored paste on dark paper, or paste and paper of a similar color.

✦ Experiment with the amount of paste used. Less paste usually makes a better print. Thicker paste gives more dimension and texture to the print, but too much will flake off of the paper.

✦ Press a piece of paper over a wet printed paper and pat together. Pull the papers apart to achieve an instant landscape. To create a different pattern, sandwich yarn, string, or lace between papers. Press together and pull apart.

✦ If you think you have a hopeless mess, crumple up the soggy paper and smooth it to dry.

✦ Spread paste on mylar for a shiny undercoating. If your paper will be handled very much, adhere a rigid backing to the mylar to keep the paste from flaking off.

✦ Add a matte acrylic emulsion to the paste to help make it waterproof, or coat the dry finished papers with a matte acrylic emulsion.

✦ Add dirt, clay, or ashes to paste for color and texture.

✦ Sprinkle wet paste paper with a photo–wetting agent to create spots.

Paste paper pattern #51 by Marie Kelzer.

Paste-paper shoes by Nancy Welch.

Sugar–vinegar paste paper is another paste–paper technique. A mix of sugar and vinegar produces a textural paper with a sparkle quite different from the traditional flour–paste method.

Sugar–vinegar paste applied over printed poster.

Basic technique

Combine ½ cup sugar with ¼ cup white vinegar for paste. Add pigment of choice until desired color is achieved.

A thin coating of the solution may be applied as a glaze over heavy weight paper, or designs scratched through the paste to reveal the underlying color of the paper. If a pattern is desired, spread the sugar paste on the paper and allow to sit for a few minutes until it will hold a design when worked with a tool. If the mixture is too thick it will resemble sandpaper and crumble off. When the mix is right the finished paper will have a slight sheen and sparkle. Find additional ideas and tools as described in Paste Paper Basic technique on pages 38–39.

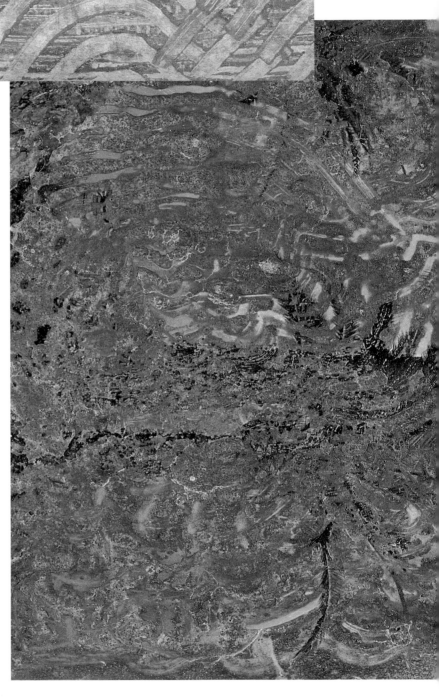

Exploring the technique

✦ Spread paste over old posters or printed papers. The color and text will peek through, adding additional dimension. *Note: Try this paste paper technique with any paste–paint recipe.*

Sugar–vinegar paste applied sparingly (above). Sugar–vinegar paste applied heavily over printed poster (right).

Plaster Paper

This is a bit like making mud–pies and just as much fun. Use heavy cardboard or mattboard for your paper surface. Depending on the texture you create and the colors you select, your piece may resemble a prehistoric wall, the bark of a tree, or a lunar landscape.

Leaf stamped with ink over dried and painted plaster paper by Melissa Slattery.

Paper with text partially embedded in plaster paper (above); basic plaster paper technique (right) by Melissa Slattery.

Basic technique

Apply a thin layer of spackle (available at the hardware store) over your paper, using a spatula or putty knife. If you desire a finer surface, substitute acrylic modeling paste for the spackle. Once the spackle has been applied to the paper you can texture it, draw in it, or make it smooth by brushing the surface with water. Shapes cut from heavy paper can be embedded into or under the spackle surface. Let the spackle dry thoroughly. You can choose to sand the surface until smooth or leave all the bumps and ridges. Color pigments, such as metallic acrylics, pastels, or whatever you have, can be rubbed into the dried surface. When color is dry, lightly rub the surface with beeswax to protect. Buff the waxed surface to add a shine.

Exploring the technique

✦ Stretch dampened paper on stretcher bars like a canvas and secure with tacks or tape. Allow paper to dry and form to stretcher bars. Apply spackle over the surface as if it were a bedroom wall to add texture.

✦ While the plaster is still wet, bits of paper or small objects can be embedded. Try creating your own graffiti wall with words and magazine pages pressed into the surface. Leaves, dried flowers, egg shells, or whatever you find are all worth embedding. Spread the spackle over some of the object edges so they disappear into the paper.

✦ Bend the spackled paper slightly to create cracks before or after it is dried. When paper surface is dried, apply color to give an aged, distressed look. Gold leaf can be applied to other areas of the surface.

✦ Apply a thick layer of spackle, then incise designs, using wood cutting tools.

✦ Rubber stamps can be used to add design to the spackle while still wet, or stamp the dried and sanded surface with ink.

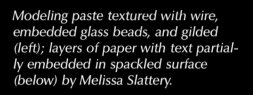

Modeling paste textured with wire, embedded glass beads, and gilded (left); layers of paper with text partially embedded in spackled surface (below) by Melissa Slattery.

Rorschach Monoprints

Basic Rorschach monoprint technique.

With this technique you have very little control over what happens, so perhaps this is the best method of all. Do this on one of those "nothing has gone right" days because this cannot go wrong. Waxed paper is used for the printing plate, along with acrylic paint. If you love glitz, add metallic paints. The only recipe for this technique is to have fun.

Basic technique

Place three or four colors of paint on the waxed paper, smear it around, draw in it, or leave the paint as is. Fold the waxed paper and press the paint around. Open up the waxed paper and place your paper surface on the paint and rub to print. Pull up the printed paper and set it aside to dry. Another print can be made by adding more paint and repeating the printing process. You can make three to four prints before the waxed paper wears out. Freezer paper will also work in place of the waxed paper, but you will not see the paint colors mingling.

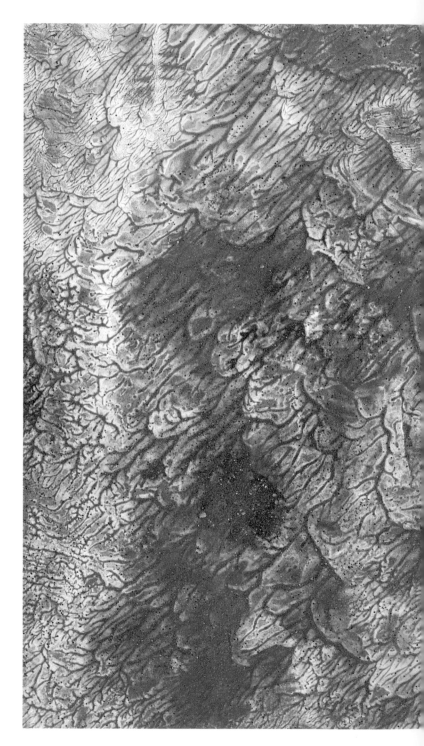

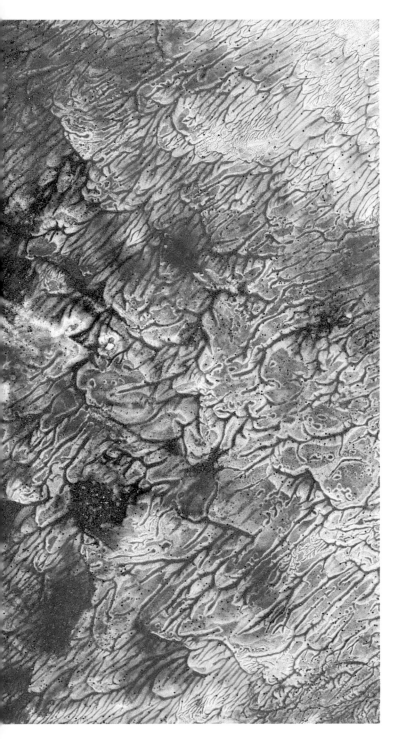

Basic Rorschach monoprint technique.

Exploring the technique

✦ Place a string in the paint before folding the waxed paper. The string may be left in the paint or pulled out to create a design.

✦ Let the waxed paper dry — it makes a shimmery, exciting paper, too.

Powdered Paper

This technique has much the same appeal as the Rorshach monoprints. Very little advanced design planning is required and the results are unique and different each time.

Basic powdered paper technique. (right and left pages).

Basic technique

Use a heavy–weight or watercolor paper and work outdoors or over a sink, because this technique is messy. Dampen your paper surface with water, then sprinkle or spill powdered paint, such as charcoal, tempera, or powdered pigment, on the paper surface. Powdered paint can be applied at random or in an organized fashion. Let paint and paper sit for a few minutes, then sprinkle water from a watering can, or gently pour water on the surface in short shots. Dry flat or lift the paper to let paint run.

Absentee Artist

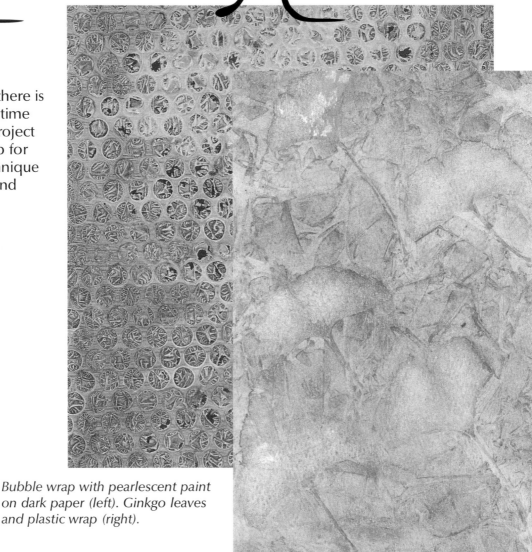

Sometimes, there is just not enough time to complete a project and still clean up for dinner. This technique lets you create and walk away.

Bubble wrap with pearlescent paint on dark paper (left). Ginkgo leaves and plastic wrap (right).

Basic technique

Select a paint or ink that is liquid and not too thick. Pour color on a heavy paper, such as watercolor paper, and cover the paper surface with crumpled plastic food wrap. Leave the pigment as is, or push and squeeze the color around under the plastic. Allow your artwork to sit overnight. When the pigment is dry, remove the plastic wrap and admire the surprising results. If you do not like the results, try pouring on another color, then cover with fresh plastic wrap and check the results when dry.

Foil and metallic paint (left). Basic Absentee Artist technique, using plastic wrap (right).

Exploring the technique

✦ Shapes cut from milk cartons or plastic lids can be placed under the plastic wrap to vary the design.

✦ Variations include sprinkling the paper surface with canning salt to form crystal patterns after the color has been applied. Cover with plastic wrap or leave to dry.

✦ Cover the wet, painted paper with other types of materials, such as aluminum foil, bubble wrap, cellophane, embossed plastics, or waxed paper, for different results.

✦ Tilt the paper as the plastic settles, to bleed one color into the next.

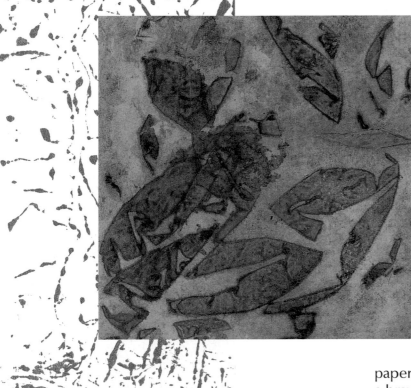

✦ Lay leaves, flowers, grass, ferns, or any flat object on moistened paper before pouring on your color. Cover with the plastic wrap. Place a board or other flat weight on the paper to maintain a direct contact between the plant material, paper, and color. Set aside until completely dry. Remove the weight, plastic wrap, and plant material to see the final results.

✦ When one layer is dry, remove the plastic wrap and pour on a lighter color, place plastic wrap on top, and allow to dry.

✦ If thicker paints are used, spread them sparingly with a brayer or wide paintbrush on crumpled aluminum foil or plastic wrap. Firmly press the paper against the foil or plastic wrap, or run a brayer over the back of the paper to pick up the print of the crumpled surface.

Faux Finishes

Many of the products used to create faux finishes on furniture are easily adapted to paper. Some are available in kits, so all you have to do is follow manufacturer's instructions. Simply pretend you are working on an antique brass bowl or a thrift store table instead of a scrap of paper.

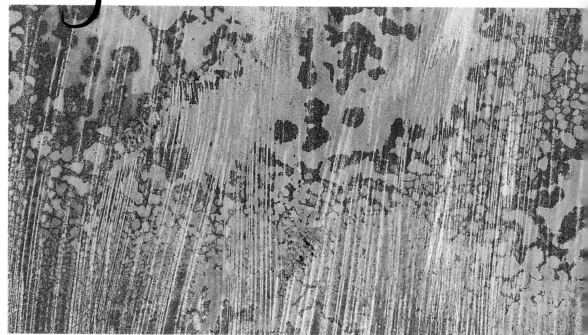

Basic technique

Create a blue or green **patina finish** that gives a verdigris finish similar to that of old brass or copper. Paint your paper with a metallic–based paint or a product that applies a "metallic" finish. When the paint is dry, apply the patina finish, using a stiff paintbrush and following manufacturer's instructions. A dull film will develop and change color as it dries. In minutes you will have a piece of paper that could be mistaken for antique copper or brass. When thoroughly dry, brush off the powdery residue. If desired, spray with a clear sealer.

Patina finish over metallic paint (left). Metallic paint over crackle medium (center). Acrylic paint over crackle medium (right).

Basic technique

Create a **crackle finish** on your paper surface by applying a coat of acrylic paint, using a flat paintbrush. Allow to dry. Follow manufacturer's instructions before applying crackle medium and second coat of paint. As medium dries, it will crackle and reveal the bottom layer of paint.

Blueprinting

With a little help from the sun, you can create art. Blueprints are the most common of light–sensitive products, but, there are other products that give a wider range of color. Blueprinting creates a negative print of an object placed over paper or fabric coated with the solution. Where the light has been blocked, the paper will remain the original color or slightly tinted by the blueprint solution. The area exposed to the sun or light will darken.

High–contrast photo blueprinted on watercolor paper by Barbara Hewitt.

Basic technique

Blueprint paper may be purchased or you can make your own blueprint solution. This technique is also referred to as cyanotype. The coated paper and the solutions must be stored in complete darkness.

Blueprint solution:

The first chemical, a crystal, potassium ferricyanide (anhydrous) can be poisonous. It is available at photography labs. The second ingredient, ferric ammonium citrate (green) is available at chemical supply laboratories. Read the labels and observe all safety precautions. Wear rubber gloves and use disposable equipment or equipment you designate to be used only for this technique.

Thoroughly dissolve 1 tablespoon of the ferricyanide in ½ cup of hot water. Use distilled water if your tap water has much chlorine in it, or if you have "hard" water. Store this solution in a lightproof container, such as a brown or amber bottle. *Note: Never use a food container, coke bottle, etc., to store craft supplies.*

Mix 2 tablespoons of the ferric ammonium citrate in ½ cup of hot water until dissolved. Store this solution in the dark, also.

The wet chemicals when stored separately, should have a shelf life of six months. The chemicals keep indefinitely in their dry state.

When you are ready to blueprint, mix equal parts of the two solutions together. The mixture is now light sensitive, so work in a low light area.

Coat the paper with the blueprint solution, either purchased or homemade, using a paintbrush. The blueprint solution will be greenish, but when exposed to sun or heat, it turns blue. Apply the solution in stripes or designs, or brush over the entire surface of the paper. Place the paper in complete darkness to dry.

Chinese paper cuts, using photo–sensitive solution.

When you are ready to develop your blueprint, place objects, such as leaves, stencils, doilies, or Chinese paper cuts — the choices are endless — on the blueprint paper surface and expose to the sun or a bright light. If it is windy or the object is lightweight, place a sheet of glass or clear, heavy plastic over the coated paper and objects to insure complete contact with the paper. The covering must be larger than the printing surface to prevent the edges from printing. Light will seep under any area that is not completely flat and cause blurred edges. If the glass has a pattern or is dirty, that will also print. The length of exposure time depends on the heat and brightness of the light. Check after four minutes in the summer, in winter it may take as long as twenty minutes to develop. Weather conditions and the distance from the equator are other factors that affect the development time. Check the development by lifting the corner of the paper carefully so as not to blur the edges and to make certain the blocked–out area remains clear. When the print has reached the desired shade, rinse the paper thoroughly in water to stop further development. Remove all the solution or your paper will continue to darken and the design will eventually disappear.

Tips/Hints
✦ Get in the habit of storing all leftover craft products out of the way and clearly marked, especially important when the materials are toxic. Doing so could prevent an accident.

✦ If you do not feel like fussing with chemicals, look for light sensitive products from photographic and art supply stores. It will not only save you the trouble of mixing, but offer a selection of colors as well.

Exploring the technique

✦ Positive prints can be made by brushing an object with blueprint or other photo–sensitive solution. Press it on an untreated paper surface to print the image. Remove the object and expose the surface to light or heat.

✦ Create an illusion of depth by coating an object, such as a leaf, and pressing it, solution side down, on untreated paper; then overlap the first leaf by pressing with another coated leaf. The first object will act as a mask, making the second print appear to be behind the first. Remove both leaves and expose the paper to bright light.

✦ Moving an image slightly during the last two minutes of exposure will give a shadow print.

✦ Use an image from a photo or magazine by selecting one with high contrast like a black and white and photocopy it to transparent acetate. Place this copy on the treated paper. Set a piece of glass over it to keep flat, and expose to bright light. Turn the acetate over to create a mirror image.

✦ Write or draw directly onto the acetate permanent markers or dark, lithographic opaque pens. Place the transparency under glass and expose as above. Images printed from the computer onto acetate will also work.

High contrast images and nature for blueprinting (left page), pine sprigs used for blueprinting (above) by Barbara Hewitt.

Brown Paper Glamour

Brown wrapping paper has been around since 1570, and is a splendid source of paper. Any number of different looks, including leather, can be created with something as simple and inexpensive as used brown wrapping paper or grocery bags.

Faux batik leather–look.

Exploring the technique

✦ Lightly cover the paper surface with black spray paint, then follow with a short burst of red spray paint. You have quickly created an elegant oriental–style paper. Paint that is old and splatters instead of lightly spraying, gives a different — but every bit as effective — finish. This technique can be done with any number of color combinations.

Red and black paint sprayed on brown paper bag.

◆ Rub wrinkled brown paper with metallic crayons. Add details with metallic pens.

◆ Scrunch paper bags by hand to make a softer, textured paper. Open the bags up and the wrinkles will form shadows when sprayed.

◆ Open the seams on a brown paper bag. Soak the paper in water to soften and squeeze thoroughly. Drop dye or ink into the folds, using an eyedropper. Scrunch the paper several times, open up and allow to dry. The final product resembles dyed batik leather.

Ink dropped on soaked brown paper (left). Metallic crayons rubbed on wrinkled brown paper (right).

Paper Dyeing

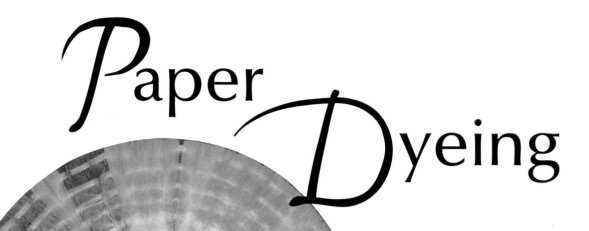

You can re-create the wild colored patterns of tie-dyed shirts on paper. Unlike fabric, dyed paper is not rinsed so it will retain the color better. Repeat patterns can be created by using folded papers.

Tie-dyed coffee filter (top). Triangle fold with corners dipped in different color dyes (bottom).

Strong, absorbent papers, preferably with no sizing, are best. Oriental rice papers — those used for sumi painting or making Shoji screens — are ideal for dyeing. Try other absorbent papers, such as paper towels, coffee filters, and good quality napkins. Experiment with dyeing absorbent, colored, or patterned papers. The density of the paper will determine how long to leave the paper in the dye bath. Paper towels and napkins that are highly absorbent need only a short dip. With less absorbent papers that respond poorly to dyeing, try one of these techniques and see which works best for the type of paper being used:

A. Crumple and soften the paper by hand before placing in the dye bath.

B. Soak the paper in water before placing in the dye bath.

C. Use a hot dye solution.

Fade-proof inks or cotton fabric dyes are best for this technique. Other dye possibilities are cold-water dyes, food coloring, Easter egg dye, watercolors, or thinned acrylics. The color in the dye bath needs to be strong as it will dry lighter than it appears. If the color is too concentrated, add water. Mix hot-water dyes with boiling water first to completely dissolve the dye powder. Tone down a bright color or create a new one by mixing two colors of dye together.

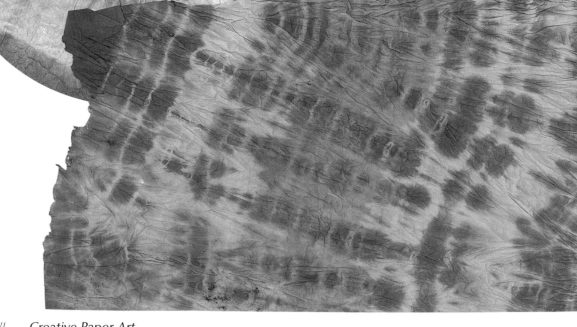

Tie-dyed paper (left and below).

Basic technique

To **tie–dye** samples, cut up squares of absorbent paper or use coffee filters for round designs. Bind with fine thread, string, old nylon stockings, or rubber bands. This serves as a resist and keeps the dye from fully penetrating the wrapped areas of your paper. A very simple way to tie–dye is to clutch a paper bundle tightly with tongs and dip it into different colors while rotating the tongs. The tongs will resist the dye and form their own pattern. Keep paper towels handy to blot your designs before redipping and to wipe up any drips. The blot papers produce artwork all on their own.

Triangle fold, with corners dipped in two different colored dyes (above). Vertical and horizontal accordion fold dipped in two different colored dyes (below).

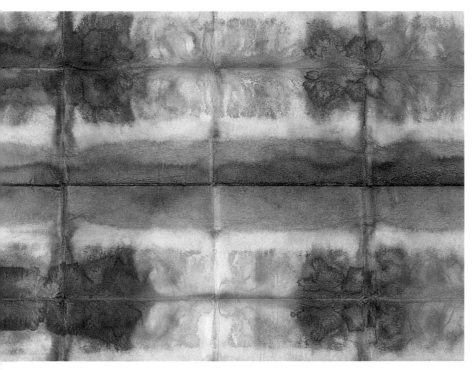

Basic technique

To **fold–dye** samples, cut up rectangles of absorbent paper. Experiment with various diagonal or accordion folds. Precise folding will give the best results. An accordion fold is one way to produce even patterns.
1. Fold paper in half lengthwise, open it up, then fold each half lengthwise to the center line. Do not unfold.

2. Turn the paper over and fold each half lengthwise to the center line. Do not unfold.

3. Fold the paper on the original fold line. You now have an accordion –folded paper with eight sections.

Secure the folded edges of long papers by placing paper clips every few inches.

To make a simple striped paper, mix your dye bath in a long pan, such as one for wallpaper or silverware. Dip only the long, folded edges into the dye.

For more complicated patterns, use the same basic accordion fold as described in steps 1–3 on page 65. After making the basic accordion fold, follow the next three steps:

1. Begin at one end and fold one corner into a right angle or an isosceles triangle.

2. Place first fold face down on the table and fold the long tail back, keeping the edges even. Repeat, folding back and forth until paper is completely folded.

3. Dip the corners into different colored dye baths.

Isosceles triangle fold, with each corner dipped into different colored dyes.

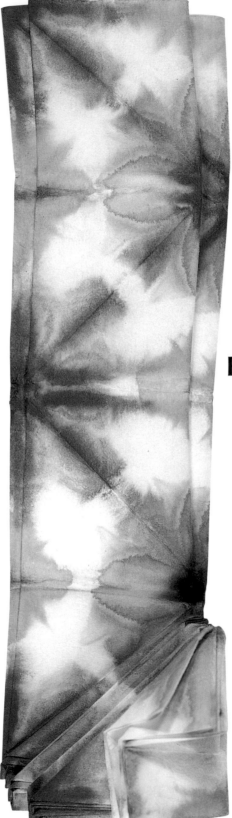

Tips/Hints:
✦ Damp paper will absorb the dye quicker.

✦ Open your dyed paper carefully so as not to tear it. If your paper begins to tear, let it dry before unfolding.

✦ Fold marks will remain as a part of this technique, but can be smoothed by ironing or weighting down the finished papers.

Basic technique

To **clamp–dye (Itajime)**, you will need to clamp a thin strip of wood or other resist material over the area you do not want dyed. Clamping materials can consist of plexiglass, wood, plastic, styrofoam, metals that will not rust, milk carton cutouts, or any other waterproof material that can be directly clamped to your paper. Cut these clamps to the shape of resist pattern that you desire, such as a square, triangle, or circle. Secure the shape to your paper, using clothes pins, rubber bands, string, or spring clamps. Dip into the dye bath. Open your paper carefully, referring to Tips/Hints on this page, and allow to dry.

Isosceles triangle fold with a shaped plastic clamp in the center of the fold.

✦ Retain the original color of the paper and create a batik–look by painting a design with melted wax and a paintbrush before dyeing. Iron wax out when the paper is dry.

✦ Quickly dip folded paper into water before immersing into dye so the colors will bleed together instead of remaining separate.

✦ To add highlights to dyed paper or for a more accurate placement of color, apply dye to the folded paper, using an eyedropper or paintbrush.

✦ Use one color but create several shades by adding additional dye to the water. Dip from the lightest to the darkest value for a monochromatic design.

✦ Crumple damp paper, smooth it out, and brush with diluted dye or drop dots of dye as desired. Allow paper to dry and iron smooth. The color takes differently at the folds and produces a mottled batik effect like the technique described in Brown Paper Glamour on pages 60–62.

✦ Dye the towels and napkins that have been used to blot acrylic paints for unusual patterns.

✦ Strengthen delicate dyed papers by adhering onto a paper backing with a thin coat of paste or spray adhesive, carefully working from the center out, and smoothing as you go. As an extra measure, run a rolling pin over the surface.

Exploring the technique

✦ Dye folded paper, leaving one or two corners undyed. Allow the paper to dry and refold. Dip the undyed area into a different color. Open the paper carefully and allow to dry.

✦ After dyeing, place the folded and dyed paper on newspaper and press firmly to distribute the color through the paper. Open your paper carefully and allow to dry.

✦ Dye folded paper, leaving one or two corners undyed. Allow the paper to dry and refold. Dip the undyed corners into water and the original color will outline the second dipping.

Japanese paper doll with fold

Cave painting with scrunched, dyed, painted, and burned paper by a Mongolian street painter.

Marbling

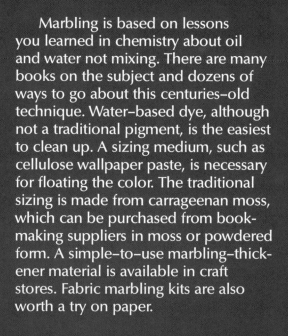

Marbling is based on lessons you learned in chemistry about oil and water not mixing. There are many books on the subject and dozens of ways to go about this centuries–old technique. Water–based dye, although not a traditional pigment, is the easiest to clean up. A sizing medium, such as cellulose wallpaper paste, is necessary for floating the color. The traditional sizing is made from carrageenan moss, which can be purchased from book-making suppliers in moss or powdered form. A simple–to–use marbling–thickener material is available in craft stores. Fabric marbling kits are also worth a try on paper.

Basic marbling technique
(left and right page).

Basic technique

Mix the sizing with water in a pan large enough to hold your paper and minimum 2" deep, following the manufacturer's instructions; or mix to a thick consistency that will still be fluid enough to allow patterns to form on the water. Let the sizing age in a cool place or refrigerate overnight. Bring to room temperature before using.

Acrylic paints diluted with water and water–based silk fabric dyes work well. Gently place a spot of pigment on the sizing mix, to test the consistency of the color. The drop should float out to a circle approximately 1" wide. It is acceptable for a small amount of color to sink as long as the majority stays on top of the sizing. If all of the pigment sinks through the sizing, you will need to dilute the pigment with water to help it float. If the color disperses too readily, add more pigment.

Once you have achieved the desired consistency, skim off the practice pigment with a piece of cardboard or newspaper before starting. Gently float drops or a line of color on the sizing. As you add more pigment, the colors will intensify where they are pushed together. Manipulate the pattern, using a feather, comb, or pointed tool, such as an old pencil, a dried out pen, a needle, or a nail. When a pattern develops that you like, carefully roll paper over the design to eliminate any air bubbles.

Lift the paper from the sizing and gently rinse under the faucet to remove any extra sizing. Air–dry the paper. Any excess pigment can be skimmed off the sizing between prints or additional pigment can be added to renew the color that is left.

Construct a marbling comb by inserting t–pins from the top down through a strip of corrugated cardboard and securing with masking tape. The points should stick out about 1½". If you plan to use the cardboard marbling comb more than a few times, seal it with varnish or acrylic medium. Substitute a wide–toothed plastic hair comb, or a tooth–shaped cutout from a milk carton. If you make the comb the same width as the marbling pan, the design will be even across the surface.

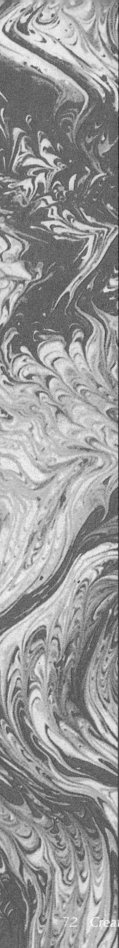

Exploring the technique

✦ Keep every sheet, even the skims from the practice paint, regardless of whether they are terrific or not. They will be great for collage, or as a background for another technique.

✦ Drop several large spots of pigment on the sizing mix. Pull a pointed tool through the center of each spot to form hearts.

✦ Try unusual color combinations manipulated with various types of tools to see what patterns develop.

✦ To create pigment–free spots in a design, drop a bit of liquid soap diluted in water, to act as a dispersant, onto the paint. Place it deliberately in a section or just flick it on randomly.

✦ If anything touches the paper while it is still wet, it will distort the pattern. Do not view this as a problem, instead create a pattern within a pattern by placing plastic, or other types of materials as described in "Absentee Artist" on pages 52-53 on the wet surface and allow to dry before removing.

✦ Try spraying paint on the sizing mix. This offers little control but it is quick. Automotive metallic paints can produce an interesting design. When using spray paints, use a disposable container.

শুভ জন্মদিন ক্যালিগ্রাফী রিভিউ

TRANSLATION:
HAPPY BIRTHDAY
TO THE GREATEST MAGAZINE IN PRINT
from Bellerophon, Dhaka, Bangladesh, 1993

Suminagashi

The European or Western way of marbling is the most familiar method; but in the 12th century, the Japanese developed a much more subtle technique called suminagashi, which literally means "spilled ink." It suggests the flowing motion of water or cloth. Traditionally, these papers were marbled in black and indigo. This technique produces soft, subtle, flowing designs.

The suminagashi technique is simple to set up. You float color pigment on a pan of water. Heavily pigmented hand–ground drawing ink called sumi comes in liquid, cake, or tube and is the traditional pigment. If you have access to a Japanese art store, you may find sumi ink in colors. Higgins Black Magic, Pelikan Black #17, or other waterproof and shellac–based inks will work if sumi ink is not available.

Second design printed over first design.

Basic Suminagashi technique.

Basic technique

Using a glass, rectangular baking dish to hold the water makes it easy to see the marbled pattern. Absorbent papers, such as blockprinting, rice, handmade, construction paper, newsprint; and even pages from old books work well.

Apply the ink to the surface of the water, using any pointed tool, such as a toothpick, pencil point, nail, watercolor paintbrushes, or the traditional oriental bamboo calligraphy brushes. Brushes hold more ink and several can easily be held in one hand to alternately dot each color to the surface of the water.

And now for that Zen moment. Pick up ink on the tip of the pointed tool or brush and lightly touch just the tip to the surface of the water. If too much ink is placed on the water, it will sink. A thin, circular film of color should begin to spread over the water surface. When you get a good film, repeat with a different colored ink or dispersant in the middle of the first ring, gradually building out in concentric circles. *Note: See Tips/Hints on page 76 for information on dispersants.* Wait patiently or blow gently across the surface of the water to create random swirls. The surface tension of the water holds the magic.

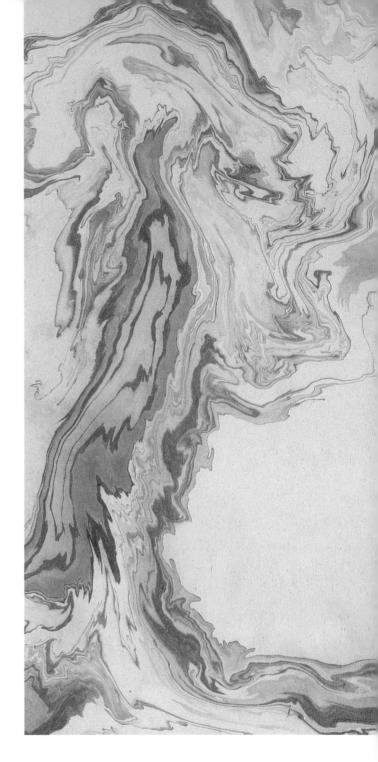

Hold your paper on opposite corners. When a pattern that you like appears, gently ease one corner, followed by the rest of the paper, diagonally across the water. Make certain there are no air bubbles trapped underneath. As soon as the pattern is captured on the paper, remove it from the water. If your paper is fragile, slip a wooden dowel or stick under one edge to help remove it from the water. Drain, or blot your printed paper with a soft rag, and air dry.

After every printing, drag a strip of newspaper completely over the surface to skim away any remaining ink. Even with careful skimming, it may be necessary to change the water frequently.

Tips/Hints:

✦ A **sumifactant** or dispersing agent is used to help the ink spread. Turpentine, aftershave, liquid soap mixed with water, suminagashi sumifactants, or a photographic wetting solution available from a photo lab are dispersants. Acrylic paint will work as a dispersant to waterproof ink. Traditionally a brush is rubbed on the side of the nose to pick up oil to act as a dispersant.

Exploring the technique

✦ Use sumifactants to create pigment–free spaces in the design. Experiment with the types of dispersants described in Tips/Hints at left. Load one paintbrush with the dispersant to leave a clear ring, and another paintbrush with the ink. Alternate to create concentric circles.

✦ Some inks disappear instantly. They will float with a tiny drop of photographic wetting solution to 1 tablespoon of ink. *Note: If too much photographic wetting solution is used, it will cause the ink to sink.*

✦ Create patterns by blowing (a straw helps direct the air) or fanning the surface gently to make the ink swirl. The stronger the air, the more jagged or broken up the lines will be.

✦ Use a bamboo skewer or a hair from your head, which is the traditional method, to draw a pattern through the floating ink.

✦ Any pigment that floats on top of the water can be used. Try water –based marking pens, fabric dye, or food coloring in place of drawing ink.

✦ Paper can be marbled several times to pick up plaid–like patterns. Let the paper dry between dipping for clearer lines.

✦ Experiment with colored paper or paper that has printed designs.

Basic Suminagashi technique (left and right page).

chapter three

Glitter, Glitz, and Dimension

Metallic surfaces are candy for the eyes, while raised or three-dimensional surfaces satisfy the tactile urges in all of us. Stroking and feeling paper may not have occurred to you before, but it will be hard to keep your hands off some of the papers.

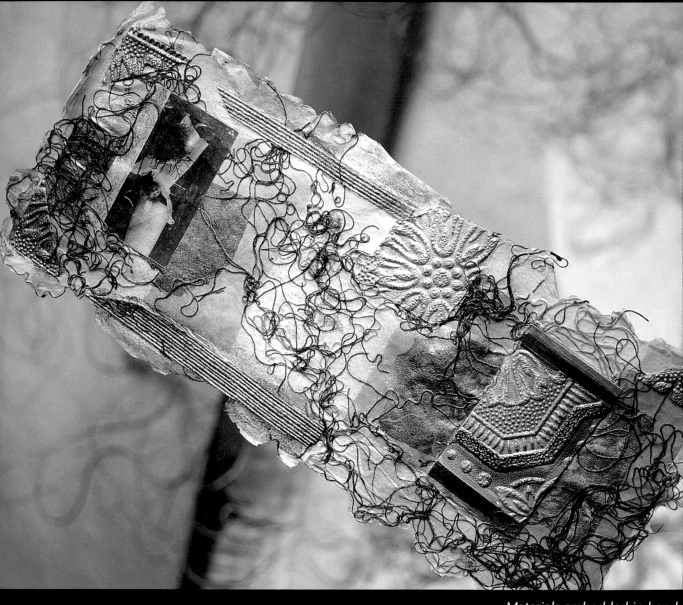

Materials embedded in hand-made paper by Nancy Welch

Gilding

Gilding is an elegant and rich way to accent a paper surface. Traditionally a thin layer of gold is applied to a surface. But, you are not limited to gold. Metallic powders, metallic paints, or gold, copper, and silver leafing add a special touch to any surface, whether it is stationery or a beautiful piece of artwork.

Layered and découpaged papers outline–gilded with metallic paint by Rhonda Rainey.

Basic technique

Gild your paper surface by using one of the following methods:

A. Brush a thin layer of craft glue where desired onto your paper. Paper with a hard surface works best. When glue dries to a tacky stage, sprinkle a small amount of metallic powder on a soft rag wrapped around your finger. Gently rub the powder over the tacky surface. Allow to dry. Buff to remove any excess powder and to produce a sheen.

B. Adhere metallic leafing to your paper surface with an adhesive, following the manufacturer's instructions.

C. Apply metallic paint, using a paintbrush, or by outline a design or pattern, using craft tips and metallic acrylic paint.

Watercolor paper gilded with metallic powder.

Crackle background with skele-tonized leaves; handmade paper; and gold and copper leaf (left) by Rhonda Rainey.

Exploring the technique

✦ To lay–out straight lines, use low–tack masking tape, or removable transparent tape to act as a guide. Rub metallic powder between the lines of tape. For other shapes and designs, attach stencils.

✦ "Antique" gilding and make it look worn by gently wiping off areas, using a slightly damp paintbrush or rag.

✦ Apply metallic leafing to desired areas on the surface, then brush a metallic acrylic paint wash over the entire paper, creating a metallic sheen.

Gilded paper on a rock paperweight by Nancy Welch.

Metallic Pens

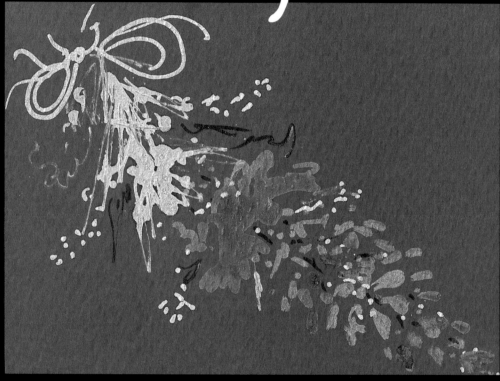

Metallic pens make it easy to add highlights to a design, write a thought, or add a fine line for a decorative touch. You are only limited by your imagination when it comes to all the possibilities and uses of metallic pens.

Basic metallic pen technique by Gail Gandolfi.

Basic technique

Shake your metallic pens until they rattle
and roll. Start by drawing on a piece of
scrap paper to get an even ink flow.
Draw straight lines, using a ruler with
slightly raised edge, so ink will not bleed
and smear under the ruler. Wherever
possible, run lines right off paper to keep
a continuous flow. If the pen tip jams or
clogs, tap vertically on nonporous paper
to release ink. The pool of ink released
can be used for redipping pen point.
Metallic pens are available containing
two colors. As you write, the pen auto-
matically outlines in a second color.

*Basic metallic pen technique
by Pauline Locke.*

Fabric and Craft Paint

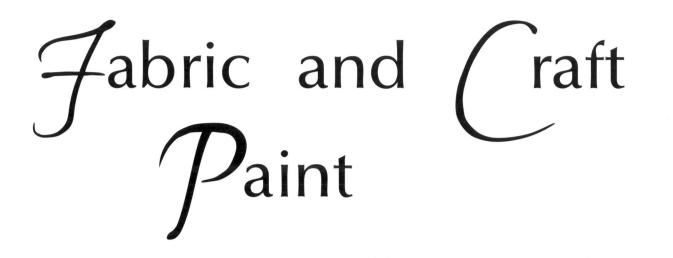

Most of the paints made for decorating fabrics or craft items will also work on paper. Numerous colors and textures are available, making them an easy way to add shine, glitter, and iridescence to your paper surfaces.

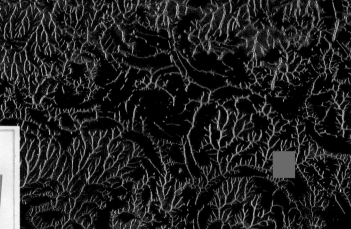

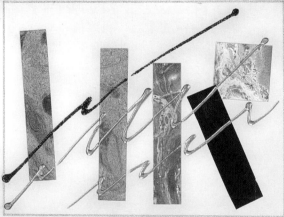

Card embellished with paper, foil, and metallic fabric paints (left) by Michiko Toyama. Fabric paint textured, using plastic bag (above) by Jan Davis.

Basic technique

Paint on scratch paper first to be certain you have a steady flow. Draw your design on the paper, using a pencil, and trace over the design with paint. If you are adventurous, paint the design freehand. Set aside and allow to dry.

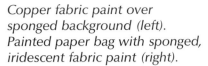

Copper fabric paint over sponged background (left). Painted paper bag with sponged, iridescent fabric paint (right).

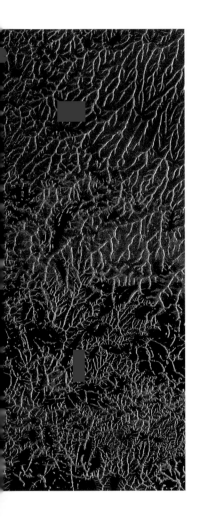

Exploring the technique

✦ Use the mud–pie approach by placing a plastic bag over your hand, dab up and down in the paint. Metallic acrylics are effective for this technique.

✦ Brushing a thin layer of metallic or iridescent paint onto the paper gives it a glimmery effect.

Thermography Powder

Thermography powder, also called embossing powder, adds sparkle and creates a raised surface on your paper. The powder is sprinkled onto a damp surface and heated until the it melts onto the paper.

Thermography powder will stick to any wet surface. Use water, ink, pigment ink pads, markers, glue, or embossing fluid as the wetting agent. It is occasionally possible to emboss the ink from some brands of copiers or printers. Sprinkle the powder on the paper as soon as the paper prints out.

Découpaged paper collage embellished with gold embossing by Rhonda Rainey.

Basic technique

Place the paper to be embossed on a larger piece of scrap paper to catch the extra thermography powder. Press rubber stamps or other printing tools on pigment ink pads or coat with embossing fluid. Either will allow you time to apply powder. Work small design areas, especially on porous paper, to keep the fluid damp. **Embossing fluid** is available at retail stores, or you can make your own solution with glycerine and water. Mix three parts glycerine to one part water. Make adjustments with glycerine or water to allow a good flow. If you plan on doing much embossing, saturate a blank ink pad with embossing fluid, or make a disposable ink pad by pouring the fluid on a folded paper towel in a waterproof container. Paintbrushes or penholder with nibs are other ways to apply the fluid to the paper.

Stamp or draw on your paper with the embossing fluid, then generously pour the thermography powder over the damp area, making certain the it adheres to the entire design. Turn the paper over the scrap paper and gently tap the back to release all surplus. Bend the scrap paper and funnel the excess back into the container. Brush off all powder that is not part of the design before heating.

Heat the area to be embossed with a heating tool that is made especially for embossing. A heat gun can be applied either to the top or the bottom. You can also heat the paper, powder side up, in an oven set at a low temperature (under 250 degrees), or over a coffee warmer until it forms a glossy, raised surface. Take care not to scorch the paper. Tongs help avoid burned fingers if you hold the paper near the heat.

Gold thermography powder on brown paper bag (top). Faux granite (bottom).

Tips/Hints:

✦ While the thermography powder is generally safe, be aware of a few precautions: Wear a dust mask when using any fine powder and wipe up spills with a damp rag. Work in a well–ventilated area. Wear safety glasses and rubber gloves as a precaution from prolonged contact. If you get any powder in your eye, flush with lots of water — do not rub. Avoid eating, drinking, or smoking while using thermography powder and wash your hands well after use. Keep this and all chemicals out of the reach of children, as you should when using any craft materials.

✦ If the powder does not melt evenly and leaves a grainy appearance, rotate your paper over the heat source until it is smooth and shiny.

✦ Thermography powders come in many colors, transparent and opaque, including white, clear, rainbow, pearlescent, metallic, tinsel, and even a (psychedelic) powder that changes colors, depending on the amount and length of heating. Pearl powders add luster to the underlying color, and tinsel adds dazzle. A clear powder allows the background to show through, which is a plus when using rainbow–colored ink pads. Most of these powders give a light impression of the underlying ink, but it is often enough to give subtle shading.

✦ Thermography powders are available from a very fine to a coarser or grainier texture. The finer powder melts quickly to a smooth veneer and the coarser makes a nice bumpy surface.

✦ Thermography powder has a tendency to cling, especially if static electricity is present. Try wiping your paper with a fabric softener sheet before applying the embossing fluid.

✦ Save small pill bottles and film canisters for storing extra powder.

Découpage with stamped and embossed embellishment by Rhonda Rainey.

Lamé–look on brown paper bag.

Exploring the technique

✦ Use two colors of thermography powder together by sprinkling a few spots with one color and tapping off the excess powder, then sprinkling the surface with the second color. *Note: Keep the excess powders separate so they can be funneled back into their containers.*

✦ Mix different colored powders together before applying to be embossed, to create an impressionist effect. If powders have been accidentally mixed, this is one way to use them up.

✦ Experiment with different combinations, such as clear, pearl, or pastel powder on colored papers. Try color–on–color, such as silver powder on silver paper or white powder on white paper. Metallic or white powders are sensational on dark paper. Try gold powder on black paper.

✦ Emboss slightly wrinkled paper with gold thermography powder to create a lamé fabric look.

✦ Clear powder mixed with a tiny amount of metallic powder adds interesting highlights.

✦ Faux finishes, like "granite," can be approximated by sponging gray paint on a glossy paper –surface in a swirl pattern. While the paint is still damp, sprinkle with white powder and heat your paper from underneath to create a pebbled surface. Finish by dabbing black ink over the surface with a dry, coarse sponge or by spattering.

✦ For a pitted lunar surface, generously apply the embossing fluid on a heavy cardstock. As the thermography powder heats, the excess liquid will bubble up, forming holes. Another way to create a pitted surface is to use one of the thicker–grained powders and heat until melted but slightly grainy.

✦ For a solid gold look, apply four or five coats of thermography powder, one over the other, on heavy paper. Apply the first layer with embossing fluid or white craft glue. Work quickly so each subsequent layer of powder will stick to the warm, melted surface of the previous layer. As the powder melts with each additional layer, it becomes molten and fluid. Objects, such as jewels or other embellishments may be embedded into the warm surface or between layers. The continued sprinkling tends to spatter around the edges of the design. Cut out the final image for a cleaner design.

Embossed envelopes by Dee Gruenig.

Groovy Paper

Paper folded and crimped.

Corrugated, crimped, or crinkled textures instantly add dimension and interest to a paper surface. Corrugate paper in a tube wringer, available at paint stores; or in a paper crimper, available at craft or scrapbook supply stores. Larger–sized wooden and metal crimpers are available from rubber stamp suppliers.

Basic technique

Corrugate a portion or all of your paper, using a commercial tube wringer or paper crimper.

Grooves can also be folded and pleated by hand. Make pleats even by marking the top and bottom of your paper into equal segments, using pencil and ruler. Score between top and bottom markings, using a blunt tool or craft knife, to make folding accurate and easy.

Create a crinkle texture by wrapping soft paper, such as brown paper bags or tissue paper, around a small–diameter dowel. Force paper down to bottom of dowel by hand. Unwrap and repeat if necessary to achieve the look you are after.

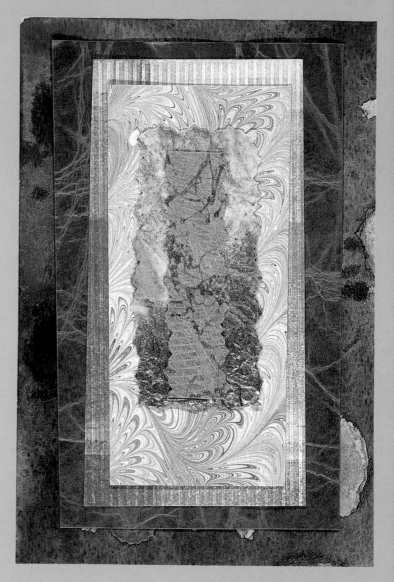

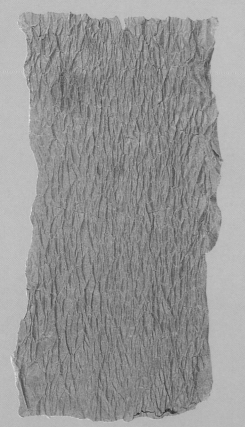

Exploring the technique

✦ Fold the paper into squares or fancy folds to fit through a small crimper.

✦ Experiment with different types of papers, such as foils, glossy, metallic, cardstock, or handmade.

Brown paper bag wrapped around dowel and crinkled (left). Various paper techniques cut and layered with one layer crinkled and gilded (right).

Corrugated paper handbag

Screen Saver

Recycle an old plastic window screen by spraying it gold and adhering it over any of your decorative papers. This is a good way to salvage a piece of paper that you thought was not successful the first time around.

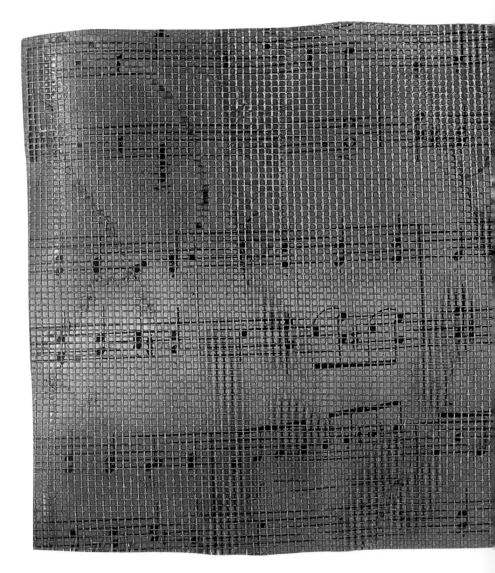

Basic technique

Use cardstock or heavier paper for this technique. Cut the plastic screen to the desired size. Spray the screen with gold paint and allow to dry. Fasten the screen to your paper with a clear–drying glue. *Note: If you would like to use a lightweight paper, adhere it to a piece of cardstock before adhering the piece of screen.*

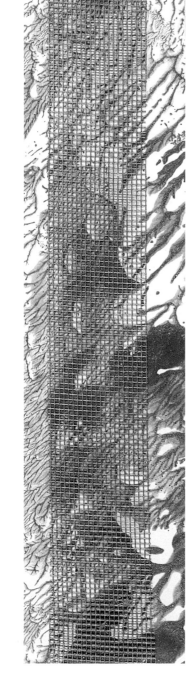

Screen over brayered background (left).
Screen on Rorschach monoprint (right).

Webbing

Webbing adds texture as well as interest to your paper surface. It comes in spray cans and can be purchased in a variety of colors at craft stores.

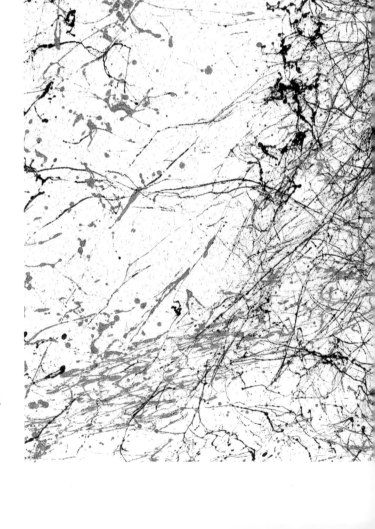

Black and gold webbing.

Basic technique

Spray webbing over plain, painted, or decorated paper. Apply as heavily or lightly as desired. Allow to dry.

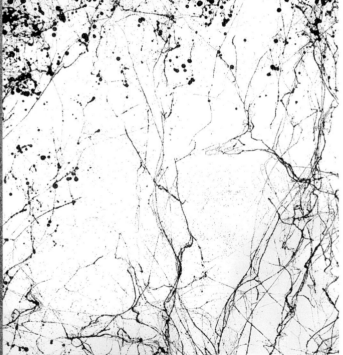

Exploring the technique

✦ Try gold of webbing sprayed over a metallic painted surface.

✦ Spray two different colors of webbing over a plain paper.

✦ Add sparkle to the paper. Spray webbing over surface, then sprinkle with glitter while still damp.

Gold webbing sprayed heavily over copper and gold metallic paint (left). Black webbing with glitter (right).

Drypoint Embossing

Drypoint embossing creates a raised or recessed surface on paper. You will need a regular stencil, a metal one made especially for embossing, or one you construct yourself — and a blunt pointed instrument, such as ballpoint burnishing tool, stylus (sold with dry embossing supplies), or cuticle stick, to press the paper into the stencil indentations.

Soft papers with a high "rag" content take impressions well and are less likely to tear than regular paper. Try recycling wedding invitations, sushi paper from a Japanese grocery store, or Tyvek® (Priority Mail) envelopes — look creatively for papers to try.

Basic embossing technique by Pauline Locke.

Basic technique

A light source will make it easier to see what is happening when you are embossing. Place the stencil on top of a light–table. Improvise one by placing a lamp under a glass –topped table or an old aquarium or stack books or boxes to support the ends of a piece of glass or thick plastic and place over a lamp. If the light source is too bright, tape tracing paper under the glass as a diffuser. Holding your stencil and paper up against a window works well during daylight. If the stencil slips or is intricate, tape it to the light source before starting. *Note: If you have a plastic or light–colored stencil, darken the edges with a permanent marker so they will show up easier.*

Place your paper on top of the stencil. Apply light pressure around the outline of the design with your embossing tool. Press toward the center with the embossing tool to gently ease the paper into the stencil design. Work slowly and carefully, because too much pressure will tear your paper.

Antique embossed envelope.

Tips/Hints:
✦ Emboss heavy papers by lightly dampening the surface that will be facing the stencil with a towel. This will help ease the paper into the stencil outline. Some will take on a shine from the rubbing. To avoid this, place a piece of tissue or tracing paper on top of the paper to be embossed.

✦ Cut stencils out of heavy acetate or mattboard by tracing a pattern with a permanent marker. Cut the pattern out, using a craft knife. If desired, adhere the pattern to a stiff backing with dry adhesive or double–sided tape. Even string can be adhered to a backing to form a design for embossing.

Embossed envelope by Julia Hierl Burmesch.

Exploring the technique

✦ Highlight embossed surfaces with pale watercolors, luminescent acrylic, a light dusting of colored chalk, pastels, or eye shadow.

✦ Add a touch of shine by lightly sponging embossing fluid on the embossed surface, sprinkle with clear or pearl powder and heat to emboss as described in Thermography, on pages 88–91.

Wet Embossing

Wet embossing adds dimension and involves a simple homemade paper–making process.

Basic wet embossing technique.

Basic technique

Gather together scraps of paper — preferably papers containing a high "rag" content, such as watercolor paper — and tear into small pieces. This technique is a great way to recycle papers. Soak the small torn pieces of paper in water until soft. Blend a small amount of paper with lots of water in a blender. *Note: Avoid overloading your blender with too much paper because it may ruin the motor.* Drain off the water and press the paper pulp into a favorite cookie mold, "cut glass" design, paper mold, or other textured surface. Work the pulp into all the mold details, with your fingers. Soak up excess water, using a sponge. Allow paper pulp to dry and remove your embossed paper.

Exploring the technique

✦ Experiment with different types and colors of paper found around the house. Tear up brown paper bags and tractor–feed printer strips or other white paper, and mix together to create an antique color.

Basic wet embossing technique.

Stitched and Sewn

Warm up the sewing machine and try stitching on paper. You can create unique and exciting designs.

Sewn and machine embroidered notecard by Jody Dufresne.

Basic technique

Stitch on decorated or plain paper. Use a
wide-stitch spacing and heavier-weight
paper that will not be apt to tear.
Experiment and play with stitching on
paper — you may never use your machine
for mending again.

*Stitched on handmade paper and pellon envelope
by Jeanine McWhorter (above left). Stitched, stamped, and
button-embellished notecard by Joanell Connolly (below).
Sponged fan and handmade paper sewn onto painted
background by Jan Davis (above right).*

Exploring the technique

✦ Try decorative stitches or freehand
machine embroidery.

✦ Stitch pieces of decorative papers
on top of each other.

Woven

Dyed, woven, and stitched paper towels by Gloria Spencer Bentley.

Woven papers can be flat or have sculptural qualities. Weave any paper that you have on hand. Try papers whose surfaces have already been treated with one or more of the techniques discussed in this book.

Woven paper with gold and silver foil by Rhonda Rainey.

Tips/Hints:
✦ Sandwich the ends of the warp strips between two pieces of paper. This will form a border, as well as a means to secure the paper.

✦ Square or rectangle edges are not your only choices. Try shaping the border either before you start or after the weaving is complete by trimming edges, and adhering cut ends to secure.

✦ Exhibit your woven paper in picture frames.

Basic technique

Cut paper into strips for weaving. Vary the width of the strips, if desired. Adhere the top of the vertical or warp strips to a paper backing to hold them in place as you weave the horizontal or weft strips through the vertical strips. When you have completed the weaving, adhere the ends of the strips to secure and hold in place.

Ribbon and Japanese paper woven and mounted on handmade paper by Marilyn Wold.

Woven basket by Linda Doherty.
Transformed paper by Nancy Welch.

Loom–woven decorative
paper weft by Bernice Huston.

chapter four

Getting It Together

If you have been practicing the techniques in this book, you should have some fabulous papers designed and be eager to show them off.

So, what are you going to do
with all this transformed paper?

Now, is the time to decide what to do with the paper you have decorated. Convert them into more than just decorative pieces by trying the following projects. Look to the gallery pictures throughout the book for additional ideas and ways to put your transformed papers to work.

Handmade paper vest with computer print and hand–dyed silk lining by Nancy Welch.

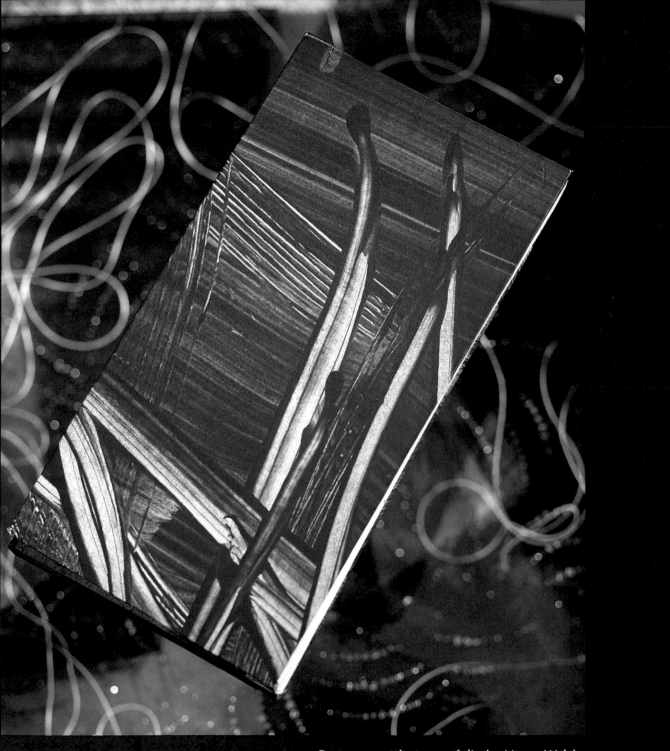

Paste paper photo portfolio by Nancy Welch.

Accordion-fold Book

Create an easy
accordion–fold book,
using lightweight
decorative papers that
you have designed
for the cover.

*Basic technique for
accordion–fold book.*

Basic technique

Cut two pieces of cardboard to desired size of book cover.

A. For the outside cover, cut two pieces of light-weight decorative paper the same length as your pieces of cardboard and twice the width plus ½". Place one piece of decorative paper face down. Place one piece of cardboard in the center of your cut paper. Fold each end toward the middle until they overlap as shown in View #1. Taper ends of paper, using scissors. Repeat, using the remaining piece of paper and cardboard.

B. For the inside of cover, cut two pieces of light-weight coordinating paper the same width as the cardboard and twice the length plus ½". Place one piece of paper face down. Place one book cover, folded ends down, in the center of your cut paper. Fold each end toward the middle until they overlap as shown in View #2. Taper ends of paper, using scissors. Tuck the folded ends between front cover and cardboard. Repeat with second cover.

C. For the pages, cut one piece of paper that is the same height as the cover and eight times the width of the cover. *Note: If you do not have paper long enough, adhere pages together at the fold slightly overlapping the pages, with craft glue.* Accordion–fold the paper to the cover size, making eight book pages. Tuck the first and last pages between the inside of the cover paper and the card-board as shown in View #3.

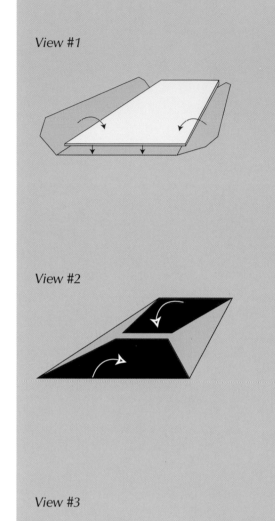

View #1

View #2

View #3

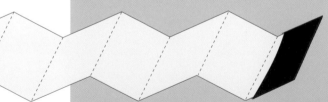

Boxes

You can make your own miniature gift boxes, or use a decorative technique on the outside of existing boxes to be used for gifts or storage for your papers and supplies.

Basic technique for miniature gift boxes.

Masking tape over a box and rubbed with shoe polish.

Exploring the technique

✦ Découpage boxes with decorative papers. Adhere bits and pieces of leftover paper to form a pleasing design.

✦ Patch a box with decorative papers as you would a quilt.

✦ Cover a box with pieces of torn masking tape. Rub shoe polish over the masking tape for a faux leather look.

Box Pattern for gift box on page 117.

Enlarge 135%

Basic technique

Make your own miniature gift boxes with paper you have decorated.
1. Enlarge gift box pattern 135%, trace pattern on decorated paper, and cut out.

2. Cut slits where indicated, using a craft knife.

3. Insert tab A into slit B to form outside of box.

4. Close top and bottom of gift box by inserting tabs C into slits D.

Bags

Decorative bags are great to have on hand for hard–to–wrap gifts. You can make wine bags, too. A handmade bag is as much a gift as the contents within.

Basic technique for bag.

Basic technique

Make small gift bags from your decorated paper:

1. Begin by using, an 8½" x 11" piece of decorated paper and two small gelatin boxes as your form. Stack gelatin boxes together and place on paper 1⅜" as shown in View #1.

2. Fold the edges of the paper over the boxes and sharp crease the corners. Adhere the paper overlap with craft glue as shown in View #2. Allow to dry.

3. Fold up the open end of the paper as if you were wrapping the ends of a gift, and sharp crease the edges as shown in View #3. Adhere flaps together with craft glue.

4. Slip the gelatin boxes out of the bag, fold in the sides of the bag, and sharp crease folds like the sides of a brown paper lunch bag as shown in View #4.

Any size gift bag can be created by selecting a form that is the desired size and shape of the completed gift bag, such as a stack of books, tall square box (for a wine bag), shoe box on end, or any other rectangle or square form. *Note: A large bag may be made by adhering two or more 8½" x 11" pieces of decorative paper with craft glue or double–sided tape along one long edge and overlapping by at least ½". Place the seam along an edge that will be folded.*

Finish the top edge of the bag by folding the edge over to the inside or the outside, or trimming the edge with decorative edge scissors. Punch holes in the folded edges and add cord handles or tie with a ribbon. *Note: Reinforce the inside bottom of the bag if necessary, by adding a decorated piece of cardboard cut to size in the bottom of the gift bag. Reinforce the hole for the handles by glueing a small piece of decorative paper inside the bag around the hole with craft glue.*

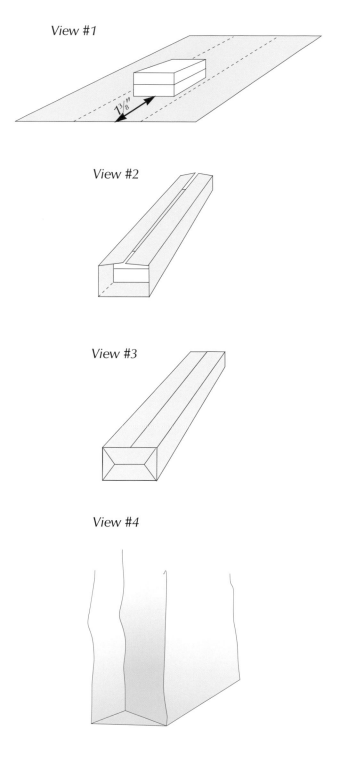

View #1

View #2

View #3

View #4

Dyed napkin bags.

Exploring the technique

✦ Dye napkins as described in Paper Dyeing on pages 63–69 and stitch edges together, forming small bags. Add cording and tassels for handles and decoration.

✦ Make a new bag out of decorated recycled grocery bags as described in Brown Paper Glamour on pages 60–62.

✦ Accordion-fold the top edge of a gift bag after contents have been placed in bag. Staple together in a fan shape and attach matching decorated paper gift card.

✦ Machine stitch with a decorative stitch to close gift bag after contents have been placed inside.

Using the Smallest Pieces

You have worked hard to produce luscious papers and will want to make use of every scrap. Even the tiniest piece can be put to use. Use these precious scraps to create a miniature book of thoughts, **jewelry**, collages, confetti, and much more.

Use tiny scraps for making jewelry. There is no limit to what you can do when creating pins, bolo ties, button covers, and earrings.

Handmade book with marbled paper closure (green book). Small accordion–fold book with paste–paper cover and ribbon and bead closure (burgundy). Miniature marbled paper thought book (peach) by Donna and Peter Thomas.

Basic technique

Make earrings quickly, by cutting out a shape from cardboard or heavy paper. Découpage tiny paper pieces onto your cut shape to create a mini collage. Allow to dry.

Protect your completed jewelry by applying a glaze or polymer gloss over the paper to seal. Adhere earring backing or punch holes and attach ear wires for drop earrings.

Paste paper earrings embellished with tiny beads (below). Miniature marbled paper book pin (center) artist unknown. Paste paper adhered to twig (right).

Exploring the technique

✦ Follow basic technique instructions and adhere a pin back or punch a hole for a necklace eyelet and cord.

✦ Make a framework from sticks. Adhere decorative paper onto the back and wire on beads.

Basic technique

Beads are a great way to rescue papers that you feel were a real flop.

A. Determine the style of beads that you wish to make and cut or tear decorated paper as shown in View #1. *Note: Adhere several layers together for thicker beads.* The length of the bead is determined by the wide end. Use a ruler and craft knife to make speedy cuts. Trim off the "ears" from wide end as shown in View #2.

B. Starting at the wide end, roll the bead as tightly as you can around a meat skewer or round toothpick as shown in View #3. *Note: If a larger hole is desired, you can roll beads over a small diameter drinking straw, leaving the straw in.* Dab a small line of craft glue along each edge up to the tip end. You need very little glue.

C. Finish beads with a coat of clear glaze, or by dipping into liquid plastic. Allow to dry.

View #1

View #2

View #3

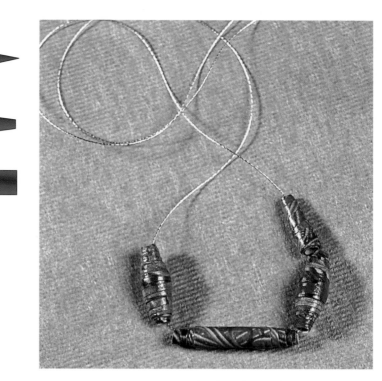

Layered and rolled beads.

Exploring the technique

✦ Roll two or three contrasting papers that have been cut or torn in various widths and layered together, starting with the narrowest piece on the outside.

✦ String paper beads in combination with other types of beads.

✦ Thread paper beads and tie together to dangle as tassels.

✦ String the paper beads on novelty yarn to add interest to a necklace.

Paper bead necklace strung on novelty yarn by Judy Content.

"The Tiny Portfolio," marbled
paper cover with ribbon and bead
closure by Diane Maurer.

Mail Order Art Supplies
The following companies offer free catalogs:

Nasco Arts & Crafts
4825 Stoddard Rd.
Modesto, CA 95356-9318
or:
901 Janesville Ave.
Fort Atkinson, WI 53538-0901
1-800 558-9595

Daniel Smith
4150 First Avenue South
Seattle, WA 98124-5568
1-800-426-6740

Dick Blick
PO Box 1267
Galesburg, IL 61402-1267
1-800-447-8192

Paper Arts
PO Box 14634
San Francisco, CA 94114
Decorative paste paper

Paper & Ink Books
15309A Sixes Bridge Rd
Emmitsburg, MD 21727

Mail Order Blueprint Supplies

Apple Tree Lane
801 La Honda Rd
Woodside, CA 94062
Dry chemicals available in sample amounts.
Send $5.00 and SASE.

Blueprints–Printable
1400 A Marsten Road
Burlingame, CA 94010
Pretreated fabric and paper for blueprinting.

Bryant Laboratory
1101 Fifth St.
Berkeley, CA 94710
Will sell chemicals in quantity.

Safety:
First and foremost, always be cautious and careful with every product and technique you try. Always read product labels for warnings and instructions.

Never use your cooking utensils for craft projects. Get in the habit of wearing a face mask when using any powders.

Do not dump unknown or hazardous substances into the sewer system.

Write to companies whose products you are using for current safety tips if you have any questions concerning their use, storage, and warnings. You can write to the following addresses for current safety tips:

Arts, Crafts, and Theater Safety
Attn: Monona Rossol
181 Thompson Street #23
New York, NY 10012

Center for Safety in the Arts
Attn: Michael McCann
5 Beekman Street,
New York, NY 10038

The Great Decorative Paper Exchange
The ideas in this book are just a starting point. It is very likely that you will come up with many variations that you may wish to share. After you create a piece of paper, cut it in quarters, write complete directions, and tape them to the back of each piece. Send your samples along with a SASE to: Nancy Welch, PO Box 620332, Woodside, CA 94062. You will get back three different samples with directions in return. This is a great way to show off your papers and see what other people are trying. Please be patient, it may take a some time to get the Great Decorative Paper Exchange started – but, you will be rewarded.

Index

Metric Equivalency Chart

¼ teaspoon	1.5 millilitres
½ teaspoon	2.5 millilitres
1 teaspoon	10 millilitres
1 tablespoon	16 millilitres
¼ cup	60 millilitres
½ cup	120 millilitres
1 cup	240 millilitres

¼ inch	.6 millimetres	0.6 centimetres
⅜ inch	.9 millimetres	0.9 centimetres
½ inch	.13 millimetres	1.3 centimetres
1 inch	.25 millimetres	2.5 centimetres